Hydroponics Gardens

Step by step guide on how to build and design inexpensive systems for growing vegetables, fruits, and herbs without soil

Table Of Contents

Chapter One: Bottle Hydroponics

Bottle Hydroponics

A QUICK GOOGLE SEARCH OF "bottle hydroponics" will uncover the numerous approaches to utilize bottles in hydroponics. Tragically, a large portion of these is either confounded, terrible, or both. These essential hydroponic bottles are anything but difficult to assemble, minimal effort, low maintenance, require no electricity and look extraordinary.

- Suitable Locations: Indoors, exterior, or greenhouse

- Size: Small

- Growing Media: Stone wool

- Electrical: Not required

- Crops: Leafy greens and herbs

Kratky Method and Aeration

The Kratky strategy is the least demanding hydroponic developing method. No pumps, no mind-boggling irrigation . . . just plants are sitting in water. A large portion of the early hydroponic research concentrated on static irrigation like the Kratky strategy. These systems worked, however, as researchers will in general do, they continued testing and in the end, discovered there was an expansion in plant development rate when the Nutrient solution was aerated. This disclosure prodded the improvement of circling hydroponic systems with expanded air circulation, similar to Nutrient film strategy (NFT) and Top drip irrigation.

Presently a large portion of the hydroponic research is centred around these circulatory systems, yet there are still horticulturists trying different things with static noncirculating hydroponics. One of the most vocal proponents of noncirculating hydroponics is Dr Bernard Kratky of the University of Hawaii. He has accomplished such a great deal to proceed with the advancement of noncirculating hydroponics that his name has gotten synonymous with the procedure the Kratky technique.

Crops

The Kratky technique has been effectively used to grow a broad scope of crops, from leafy greens like lettuce to blossoming crops like tomatoes and potatoes. Most hydroponic plant specialists want to develop leafy greens and herbs with the Kratky technique in light of the fact that the bigger crops may battle with lacking oxygen levels in their root zone. The root zone oxygen interest for crops like lettuce is opposite short of what it is for tomatoes.

The crops that are best for bottle hydroponics remain short or develop upstanding to alleviate the chance of the system getting too Top-heavy and falling over. Basil, kale, Swiss chard, and lettuce are my Top choices for bottle hydroponics, yet additional accomplishment has been made with cilantro, dill, and different herbs.

Locations

The Kratky technique can be utilized exterior, inside, or in a greenhouse. It might be hard to use a Kratky-style garden exterior in territories with substantial precipitation in light of the fact that the Nutrient solution might be immediately weakened or washed away. Kratky-style gardens are incredible for off-grid gardens that don't access electricity.

The proper locations for bottle hydroponics are progressively restricted. The dark paint utilized right now lead to over the Top warmth development in the root zone. If you need to use bottle hydroponics exterior, you'll need to use a light-hued paint for regions with warm atmospheres. My preferred method to utilize bottle hydroponic systems exterior is with a wall-mounted bottle holder on a porch. This keeps the Bottles in a semi-concealed territory, and it looks marvellous. Inside, bottle hydroponics can be set about anyplace—a kitchen counter, work area, windowsill, or even divider mounted in a passage with a develop light above the main constraining element while setting a bottle hydroponic system inside its access to light.

MATERIALS & TOOLS

Required

Glass or plastic bottle

Stone wool seedling plug measured for bottle opening

Fertilizer

Optional

Scotch tape

Stake for mounting while at the same time painting

Chalkboard shower paint

Chalk

Burlap or cloth

Bottle mark

Grow light

Optional Tools

Scissors Funnel

Hot glue gun

Bottle Preparation

The bottle choice is the essential choice right now. The perfect bottle has a short neck so the plug can rapidly get to the primary body of the bottle. If conceivable, select a wide bottle. Wide bottles keep up their water level longer, giving the roots a higher chance to develop into the Nutrient solution before the water level drops because of evapotranspiration. The accompanying advances are for clear bottles.

1. Remove any names from the bottle.

2. Add a portion of tape at the frame. This will be evacuated later to make a review window for the roots. Overlap the finish of the tape strip on the base of the bottle to make evacuation simpler in the wake of painting.

3. My favoured technique for painting bottles is putting them on a stake; however, I've additionally had achievement plunging bottles in the paint. Ensure there are sufficient layers of paint that light won't enter inside the bottle.

4. Remove the tape strip once the paint dries.

5. It is ideal to do any chalk art now before filling the bottle with water.

Plug Selection

Either select a plug that fits cosily in the neck of the bottle or choose a bottle with an opening appropriate to your caps. It is conceivable to slice a stone wool plug to fit a littler bottle yet this can possibly harm the seedling's foundations.

6. The plug ought to be sufficiently broad to hold itself solidly in the opening of the bottle.

7. Growing a bigger number of seedlings than required permits you more prominent choices to choose simply the best seedlings for your hydroponic bottle.

Nutrient Solution and Transplanting

It is critical to utilize manure intended for hydroponic gardens. Right now used FloraNova Grow; however, there are numerous different alternatives. Look at the Plant Nutrition part to get familiar with hydroponic manure choices.

8. Mix fertilizer with water utilizing the suggested rates recorded on the manure bottle or sack. Blend the water and manure in a different holder to make it simple to check if the fertilizer has completely broken down. Additional Nutrient solution might be put something aside for half a month whenever put away in a hermetically sealed compartment in a dull, cool condition.

9. Fully fill the bottle with a Nutrient solution. There is potential for some flood when the seedling is embedded; however, this is desirable over too little water.

10. If you don't anticipate utilizing a wicking strip (see next page), the seedling would now be able to be transplanted into the bottle. The base of the plug ought to be sitting in Nutrient solution; if necessary, add progressively Nutrient answer to ensure the plug is completely soaked. Ensure the bottle is totally full If you are not utilizing a wicking strip in light of the fact that the plug will require access to the Nutrient answer for a few days until it can develop roots profound into the Nutrient solution. The plug ought not to be set excessively profound into the neck of the bottle. You should evacuate the cap to Top off the bottle, so keep enough of the plug exterior of the bottle to make expulsion simple later on.

11. Check to check whether the plug is dry during the main week. Contingent upon crop choice and condition, you may need to include progressively Nutrient solution in the initial not many days to allow your plant to develop attaches sufficiently long to pull up water from the bottle. A wicking strip isn't fundamental; however, it will help lessen the Potential of your seedling drying out in the first week.

Optional Wicking Strip

A wicking strip is helpful in bottles that are tall and thin or with crops that develop gradually. The accompanying advances utilize a reasonable bottle for showing purposes, however using an unmistakable bottle for growing a plant isn't suggested on the grounds that it will electricity green growth development.

12. Cut burlap or fabric into a strip sufficiently long to arrive at the base of the bottle and around as wide as the seedling plug (generally 1" to 2" wide).

13. String the wicking strip through the bottle opening.

14. Use the seedling plug to hold the wicking strip set up.

15. Leave enough stone wool presented to make evacuation simple when Topping off the bottle with a Nutrient solution.

16. A pipe can make it conceivable to Top off the bottle without completely expelling the stone wool plug. This can help lessen the Potential of harming roots while evacuating and reinserting a plug with a created root system.

17. If not utilizing a pipe, cautiously lift the plug out of the bottle.

18. Fill the bottle with a Nutrient solution. For young plants with inadequately created roots, it is ideal to fill to about the highest point of the bottle. For more established plants with bigger root systems, it is perfect to fill to three-fourths full, so the roots approach an equalization of air and Nutrient solution.

Carefully reinsert the plug go into the bottle in the wake of Topping off. Ensure the roots are submerged in the Nutrient solution.

Support

The vast majority of the crops that are plug for hydroponic bottles are quickly developing and may not require a great deal of support during their development cycle. It is conceivable to formulate longer-term crops that have numerous crops, for example, basil, as long as the bottle is kept over half full with Nutrient solution. It is a decent practice to wipe out the bottle and Top off with crisp Nutrient solution consistently to maintain a strategic distance from Nutrient awkward nature in the solution.

Additional Options

Improvements Besides chalk craftsmanship, I like to brighten my hydroponic bottles with unofficial IDs and burlap scarfs. Covering the neck of the bottle with a scarf can help shroud any potential green growth development on the exterior of the seedling plug. I utilize a Hot glue gun to verify burlap on the neck of the bottle.

Lighting Hydroponic bottle gardens are most appropriate for inside. They can be put on a windowsill and get regular light or put under a develop light. Hydroponic bottles under a little develop light are an extraordinary expansion to a work area.

Troubleshooting

Plants are shrinking

• Check water level and include an extra Nutrient solution if the water level is low.

• Water temperature or air temperature might be excessively high.

• Try adding wicking strip if roots are not arriving at Nutrient solution.

Plug is falling into bottle

• Try enveloping plug by fabric or burlap to make a snugger fit into the neck of the bottle.

• Place plug, so increasingly stone wool is uncovered above bottle opening.

Plant is developing gradually or ineffectively

• The crop determination may not be a plug for hydroponic bottle garden.

• Crop may not be getting enough light.

• Use a fertilizer intended for hydroponics.

Chapter Two: Floating Raft/Wicking Bed

Floating Rafts

Floating Raft hydroponics is a subtype of profound water culture (DWC) hydroponics. Most customary DWC systems hold the plant at set tallness, and the Nutrient solution is Topped off to keep in touch with the roots. Floating raft hydroponics permits the plant to stay in contact with the Nutrient solution even as the water level drops. Floating Raft systems require almost no work and Maintenance. It is entirely expected to not play out any support on the system, not in any event, including water, from transplant to Assemble when developing leafy greens.

• Suitable Locations: Indoors, exterior, or garden

• Size: Small to enormous

• Growing Media: Stone wool seedling solid shapes

• Electrical: Optional

• Crops: Leafy greens and herbs

Crops

Floating Raft hydroponics has been utilized for massive blossoming crops like tomatoes, yet it is generally plugged for shorter crops with lower oxygen necessities in their root zone.

Conventional DWC systems are extraordinary for these bigger blooming crops since they make space for the roots to get to air, and they regularly use vacuum apparatus to circulate air through the Nutrient solution intensely.

I've trialled many crops in floating rafts, and I'm astounded at the adaptability of this developing strategy. The sidebar on the following page records a few crops that can be developed in floating rafts.

Locations

Floating Raft gardens can be set inside, outside, or in a garden. The exterior may have issues if not shielded from a downpour. The water will weaken the Nutrient solution and wash away the Nutrients. Floating raft systems frequently hold a great deal of water, and this probably won't be perfect inside. If the system isn't appropriately set or worked, there could be potential for breaks and flooding inside. Water is exceptionally overwhelming as well, so Floating Raft systems ought not to be Installed on floors with weight restrictions.

Floating Raft systems profit by air circulation. However, for most crops, it isn't vital. I've developed excellent heads of lettuce and basil in Floating Raft gardens with no air circulation in 90°F climate. These crops will profit by air circulation, regularly with quicker development and decreased potential for root ailments and Nutrient issues, yet floating raft gardens can flourish without electricity. There are moderate alternatives for sun based controlled Air Pumps If you wish to keep your Floating Raft garden off-matrix yet get the advantages of air circulation.

SIZING

Floating raft systems can be intended for frames or enormous fields. Extremely little floating rafts have the probability of getting temperamental when supporting enormous, Top-overwhelming crops, yet they are extraordinary for leafy greens. Floating rafts are fit for holding more weight, yet they ought to be manoeuvred when they are holding overwhelming adult crops since they can break under the weight when lifted out of the Reservoir. Most Rafts are produced using 2 × 4-foot froth boards or 4 × 8-foot froth boards cut down the middle.

Most floating raft gardens are hence rectangular with widths in additions of 2 feet and lengths in augmentations of 4 feet. Try not to feel constrained to square shapes; however; these froth boards can be sliced to any form. I've seen round kiddie pools changed into Floating Raft gardens with froth boards slice to estimate.

Great

- Basil

- Celery/celeriac
- Chives
- Dill
- Fennel
- Kale
- Lettuce
- Mustard greens
- Nasturtium
- Sorrel
- Swiss chard
- Watercress

not optimal, but possible

- Arugula
- Beets
- Carrots
- Cilantro
- Dwarf peppers
- Dwarf tomato
- Marigolds
- Mint
- Parsley
- Radishes
- Spinach
- Strawberries

Materials & Tools

Reservoir

4   2 × 12" × 8' stumble

2 1 × 2" × 8' furring stripboard

1 gal. White water-based latex

primer, sealer, and stain blocker (KILZ 2 LATEX)

1 lb.   #10 × 2½" exterior screws

1 lb.   #8 × 1¼" exterior screws

1   6 × 100' dark 6 mil.

plastic sheeting

Protection Equipment

Work gloves

Eye protection

Raft

1   1" × 4 × 8' protection froth board

18   2" net pot

Optional

18–72 2" net pots (extra

pots to build planting thickness)

1   Air pump with air stones

1   Small water pump with

venturi connection

Tools

Round observed

Paint roller and additionally paintbrush Rafter square

Level Drill

Boring apparatus coordinating screws Staple firearm and staples Heavy-obligation scissors Razor cutting frame blade Sawhorses with cinches Tape measure

Permanent marker

2" gap boring tool (if utilizing net pots)

Assemble the Reservoir

There are numerous approaches to make reservoir Assembleing simpler. Most reservoirs that sell lumber offer to slice the Lumber to explicit measurements whenever mentioned. Request the dimensions recorded in the means beneath to avoid crafted by cutting the wood and diminish the number of tools required. It is conceivable to purchase pre-assembled supplies for Floating Rafts; look at the Pots and Trays area in the Equipment part to see a portion of the alternatives.

1. Wearing work gloves and eye protection, cut the four 2 × 12" × 8' boards into the accompanying lengths:

One board into 4'4" and 2'4" segments

Another board into 4'4" and 2'4" segments

One board into 2'1", 2'4", and 2'4" segments

One board into 2'1" and 2'4" segments

Cut a 4'1" and a 2'4" segments from every one of the two 1 × 2" × 8' furring strips. Last lengths and amounts of cut Lumber:

2	2 × 12" × 4'4" boards
5	2 × 12" × 2'4" boards
2	2 × 12" × 2'1" boards
2	1 × 2" × 4'1" strips
2	1 × 2" × 2'4" strips

The Lumber can be painted before or after Assembling.

2. Lay the five 2 × 12" × 2'4" boards on a level surface. These boards will be the base of the system. It is conceivable to fabricate the reservoir frame without a base; however, a strong wood base can add a great deal of solidarity to the structure. A base additionally decreases the opportunity of tears to the reservoir liner. Froth boards are additionally regularly utilized as a base to shield the liner starting from the earliest stage.

3. Set up one of the 2 × 12" × 4'4" boards on its side running along the long side of the base and one of the 2 × 12" × 2'1" boards on its side running along the short side of the base. The 4'4" board should cover the finish of the 2'1" board.

Ensure they are square and level. Utilize two 2½" screws to secure the boards together.

4. Place the other 2 × 12" × 4'4" board along the other long side of the base and secure to the exterior finish of the 2'1" board from stage 3 utilizing two 2½" screws.

5. Place the staying 2 × 12" × 2'1" board on the last open side of the base between the two 4'4" boards. Secure into place with two 2½" screws on each end.

6. Flip over the frame and spot the five 2 × 12" × 2'4" baseboards again into position. Attach the base to the casing with two 2½" screws on each finish of the 2'4" boards.

7. Flip the housing back finished.

8. Adding the liner is one of the most troublesome strides in Assembling the reservoir. It is in every case best to have overabundance liner inside the reservoir as opposed to making the liner extremely tight. A rigid liner might be worried by the heaviness of the water and could tear, making spills. For this reservoir, I utilized two layers of 6 mil. Plastic to include some break protection. Overlay the liner at the reservoir corners to get the liner flush with the frame. When the plastic is set up, staple it to the frame of the reservoir frame.

9. Cutaway overabundance liner with scissors or an extremely sharp frame blade.

The furring strips are attached along the frame of the Reservoir to conceal the parts of the bargains liner and to hold the liner safely set up. The furring strips are not totally vital for the usefulness of the reservoir yet they include a great deal stylishly. Secure the furring strips into place with 1¼" screws.

Assemble the Raft

Building a DIY Raft is extremely simple. There are pre-assembled Rafts accessible; however, they can be costly. A significant number of the pre-assembled Rafts have openings made for explicit seedling plug estimates and wipe out the requirement for net pots. It is conceivable to make a DIY Raft with gaps explicit to your plug size, making net pots pointless, however, for this Floating Raft garden, I'm utilizing net pots since they make the procedure opposite simpler. The pre-assembled Rafts have a couple of other plan highlights, as raised plug holders, that make them extremely pleasant to utilize, yet for most applications, a DIY Raft is more than adequate.

11. Cut a 2 × 4' segment from the 1" × 4 × 8' froth board utilizing a disposable cutter blade. Brush away any free froth pieces from the cut frame.

12. Place the 2 × 4' segment of froth board on sawhorses and affix into place with clamps.

13. Most leafy greens are developed with 6" dividing in hydroponic systems. A 2 × 4' Raft with 6" separating holds 18 plants (3 columns of 6). A few greens, for example, romaine and basil, develop upstanding and can be developed at a thickness of 36 plants for each 2 × 4' Raft. A few cultivators go much higher thickness (72 plants or more for each 2 × 4' Raft) to develop crops like child kale, infant lettuce, spring blends, and a few herbs. Measure and imprint the plant site positions on the Raft and drill 2" openings with the 2" gap boring apparatus.

14. Some hydroponic producers leave the intelligent surface on their DIY froth boards, yet I lean toward the appearance of clean whiteboards in my perfect white Reservoir.

15. Test to check whether the Raft fits in the reservoir. Make any additional changes to the Raft size, so it easily fits inside the Reservoir. An excess of uncovered reservoir surface can generate electricity green growth development, yet excessively cosy of a fit makes it hard for the Raft to move descending as the water level drops after some time.

16. Place the 2" net pots into the 2" gaps in the Raft.

Including Nutrient Solution, Aeration, and Transplanting

Fill the reservoir with water to 1¼-inch underneath the beginning of the furring strip. This will be around 10-inch deep of water, roughly 50 gallons.

Utilize hydroponic manure at the suggested rate on the fertilizer bottle or pack. Blend the fertiliser into the water altogether until completely broken down.

Optional: Adding a pneumatic machine can improve plant development and lessen the danger of root spoil. The pneumatic machine to one side of the reservoir is a four-outlet 15 litres/minute pump that is associated with four 4-inch round air stones dispersed uniformly in the reservoir. This vacuum apparatus gives incredible air circulation. The littler vacuum apparatus put on the Top frame of the reservoir is associated with a little sun electricity board. This small pump has one outlet and gives all things considered one-fourth the crop of the bigger vacuum apparatus, and just in ideal conditions with full sun. A sun based controlled vacuum apparatus is progressively costly, yet it can give the advantages of air circulation without an electric bill, and the system can be set anyplace with daylight.

Float the raft in the reservoir and transplant your seedlings. Stone wool seedlings work extraordinary right now about any hydroponic substrate will work in a floating raft garden. Substrates that hold a great deal of water like coco or peat plugs will require more consideration since they may have overwatering issues when the plant is youthful with a little root system. A few producers even use seedlings began in the soil in their floating rafts. Soil-began seedlings can be muddled and may require increasingly visit cleaning of the garden; however, they are a choice.

Maintenance

Most leafy greens can be developed right now transplant to Assemble with no support of the system. For longer-term crops, see the Nutrient solution the board procedures itemized in the System Maintenance part.

Additional Options

This Floating Raft garden is utilized as a reservoir in the DIY Nutrient film procedure (NFT) system later right now. For this NFT add-on, a casing was developed to hold PVC pipes over the Raft garden. This frame likewise underpins a 4-foot six-tube T5 develop light that goes about as a Nutriental light source in extra to common daylight present in the garden. If this system were put inside, this equivalent 4-foot six-tube T5 develop light would be equipped for giving all the light required by these crops.

Troubleshooting

roots are developing ineffectively or are darker and soft

• Water might be excessively warm.

• The pH might be out of target extend. Test and modify dependent on target pH for your crop (see the informative Nutrient for target pHs).

• May have root illnesses present and electricity on fewer crops. Flush and totally clean Reservoir, Raft, and net pots before replanting the garden.

plants are developing gradually

• Check EC to ensure it is in target run.

• Garden may not be getting enough light.

• Water might be excessively cold. Temperatures under 65°F can slow development on certain crops. Have a go at painting the reservoir dark, including a water warmer, as well as choosing various crops that are increasingly tolerant of cold conditions.

water level is dropping quick

• May have a hole in the liner. Check for water around the Reservoir. If the reservoir is spilling, evacuate existing liner, check for any articles that may have caused a cut in the liner, and Nutrient another liner. If holes endure, have a go at including froth boards side dividers and the base of the reservoir before adding the new liner.

Wicking Bed

WICKING BED GARDENS ARE VERY flexible and can be adjusted for a variety of substrates, fertilizers, and crops. Like the past hydroponic gardens right now, wicking bed garden requires no electricity. The plan is incredibly simple.

Wicking beds exploit slim activity, a characteristic wonder by which water can flow upward against gravity by utilizing its surface strain and bond. A typical example is a paper towel wicking water upward from a cup. In a wicking bed garden, the "cup" is the frame of a raised bed garden and the "paper towel" is a fine-finished substrate like coco, peat, or soil.

• **Suitable Locations:** Outdoors or garden; can be changed for inside

• **Size:** Small to enormous

• **Growing Media:** Expanded mud pellets and coco coir chips

- **Electrical:** Not required

- **Crops:** Leafy greens, herbs, strawberries, and short blooming crops

The frame of a wicking bed is fixed with a waterproof layer, similar to 6 mils. Painter's plastic, to forestall spills and to shield the wood frame from decaying. The base of the bed is loaded up with a speedy draining substrate like clay pellets, waterway rock, or washed rock. The bottom of the bed holds water or a Nutrient solution that is underhanded up to the fine-finished substrate above. A texture boundary like burlap or cloth keeps the substrate from dropping into the water reservoir space. An inlet pipe makes filling the reservoir easy, and an overflow pipe prevents overwatering.

Crops

Crops that are tolerant of wet conditions are incredible for wicking bed gardens. This system may not be suitable for prickly plants. It is conceivable to structure wicking beds with a few layers of various finished substrate to make drier conditions while keeping up enough dampness for roots. However, it might include some tinkering to make sense of the best blend for your particular condition, crop determination, and garden size.

Regularly it is the size of a wicking bed garden that points of confinement crop determination. A wicking bed garden like the one portrayed in the bit by bit guide could grow an enormous blooming crop like tomato or cucumber, yet the constrained size of the garden would almost certainly limit it to only one plant.

Locations

Wicking bed gardens are ordinarily utilized exterior or in gardens. By adding a variety bottle to catch floodwater or guiding flood to a sink channel, a wicking bed garden could be used inside without making huge wreckage. The structure that follows doesn't require immediate the flood into a holder and would not be suitable inside except if altered.

Wicking System Variations

The wicking bed configuration is extremely adaptable and is seen in both hydroponic and customary gardens. The plan in the bit by bit guide can be altered to utilize usual preparing blends and fertilizers that would not be appropriate in other hydroponic garden structures. The following are a couple of Optional changes you can make to the wicking bed configuration to make it your own.

Optional Modifications

- The bay and flood channel can be produced using PVC rather than vinyl tubing.

- The frame could be a metal trough or plastic tote rather than wood with a liner.

- A lake liner could be utilized rather than painter's plastic.

- The exterior could be painted as opposed to using beautifying wood.

- A wood trellis could be based on to help bigger crops.

- A raised Rafter could be Installed over the developing bed to help a develop light.

MATERIALS & TOOLS

Frame

2	1 × 8" × 8' pine whitewood board (genuine measurements ¾" × 7¼" × 96")
5	½ × 4" × 4' endured hardwood board 1
lb.	#8 × 1¼" exterior screws
1 lb.	#8 × ¾" wood screws
1	6 × 100' dark 6 mil. plastic sheeting
2'	¾" dark vinyl tube
1	¾" fill/channel plug with screen
1	¾" tee
1	2 × 6' burlap

Protection Equipment

Work gloves

Eye protection

Substrate

10 L   Expanded clay pellets

2 cu. Ft. Coco coir chips

Optional

Chalkboard paint Paintbrush

Snappy set clear epoxy Chalk

Tools

Circular saw Rafter square Level

Drill

Drill bit coordinating screws

Tape measure

Permanent marker

1⅜" gap saw drill bit

Step drill bit with ⅛."

increases from ¼" to 1⅜."

2" gap saw drill bit Staple

firearm and staples

Heavy-obligation scissors

Sawhorses with clasps

Razor-sharp frame blade

Assemble the Frame

There are a few different ways to make frame assembly simpler. Most reservoirs that sell lumber offer to slice wood to explicit measurements whenever mentioned. Request the dimensions recorded in the means underneath to skirt crafted by cutting the Lumber and lessen the number of instruments required. The endured hardwood is utilized only for feel and could be jumped to make Assembleing simpler.

1   Wearing work gloves and eye insurance, cut the two 1 × 8" × 8' boards into the accompanying lengths:

• One board into four 18" segments and one 14½" segments

- The other board into one 14½" portion and one 19½" segments

2   Cut the five ½ × 4" × 4' endured hardwood boards into the accompanying lengths:

- Two 19½" segments and one 8¼" segments from every one of four 4' boards

- Four 8¼" segments from the other 4' board Final lengths and amounts of cut Lumber:

4   1 × 8" × 18" boards

2   1 × 8" × 14½" boards

1   1 × 8" × 19½" board

8   ½ × 4" × 19½" endured hardwood boards

8   ½ × 4" × 8¼" endured hardwood boards

3. The Top frame of the raised bed frame can be painted previously or after assembly with writing slate paint. This is absolutely a tasteful expansion, and this progression isn't important for the usefulness of the garden. If painting the frame before assembly, paint the wide frame of two 1 × 8" × 18" boards and the finish of both 1 × 8" × 14½" boards.

4. Making sure the boards are square and level, secure the finish of one 1 × 8" × 14½" board to the 1 × 8" × 19½" board utilizing two 1¼" screws. The 19½" board is the base of the casing.

5. Fasten a 1 × 8" × 18" board to the 1 × 8" × 14½" board utilizing two 1¼" screws.

6. Fasten another 1 × 8" × 18" board to the 1 × 8" × 14½" board to finish another side divider.

7. Repeat stages 5 and 6 to Assemble the opposite side divider.

8. Fasten the staying 1 × 8" × 14½" board to finish the last mass of the casing.

Install the Liner and Drainage Assembly

9. Measure and mark a gap with an inside 6" over the base of the frame and 3" from the side divider. Utilize the 1⅜" opening saw drill bit to make the gap.

10. Use the progression boring tool to create a slant around the hole outwardly of the casing. This slant is vital to append the fill/channel plug safely.

11. A line within the housing with 6 mil. Plastic. Overlay the plastic sheet at the corners to shape it to the frame.

12. Staple the plastic liner along within upper frame of the casing to hold it set up.

13. Cut out the abundance of plastic sheeting with scissors.

14. Assemble the waste funnel. Append a 3" bit of ¾" vinyl tubing to the fill/channel plug. Unscrew the clasp yet keep the elastic gasket on the plug.

15. Create a little opening in the plastic liner in the waste gap. The opening in the liner should fit tight around the plug.

16. Attach the waste funnel to the frame. Firmly screw on the latch to make the plug watertight.

17. Test the seepage pipe before continuing! Ensure there are no breaks. If breaks are found around the plug, change the liner and fix the attach. If cracks are located somewhere else, evacuate and supplant the liner. Try not to continue with spills; water should just deplete from the channel pipe.

Make the Decorative Weathered Hardwood Exterior

Including the endured hardwood exterior is Optional. This system would likewise look extraordinary painted. During the assembly of the hardwood exterior, I coincidentally cut the side boards 1 inch short. I extemporized an answer by including long thin bits of hardwood to fix in the corners. The measurements utilized in these guidelines have been rectified so you won't commit a similar error or on the other hand, innovative style loads of approaches to take a gander.

18. Use the 2" gap saw boring apparatus to make an opening in one of the 19½" segments of endured wood. The focal point of the opening ought to be 3" from the finish of the board.

19. Attach the endured hardwood to the casing.

Alternative 1: Use fast set clear epoxy and hold boards set up with clips while the epoxy dries.

Alternative 2: Use ¾" wood screws to tie down boards to frame.

Install the Inlet Pipe and Substrate

20. Assemble the bay funnel. Append an 18" bit of ¾" vinyl tubing to the ¾" tee.

21. Prepare the substrate.

22. Rinse the extended mud to wash off fine clay particles.

23. Soak the coco chip square to grow it.

24. Position the tee end of the channel pipe as an afterthought inverse the seepage pipe. The Irrigation water will enter the delta funnel and afterwards Flow over the base of the bed and channel from the channel pipe at the opposite end. Fill the bottom of the bed with clay pellets while situating the channel funnel to hold it set up.

25. Fill the bed with clay pellets until the seepage pipe is mostly secured. Try not to cover the seepage pipe excessively profound or the system will deplete before the upper degree of substrate approaches to water.

26. Cut an area of burlap sufficiently enormous to cover the developing bed. This will be the texture divider between the lower reservoir and the upper substrate. With extremely permeable textures like burlap, it is useful to utilize different layers to keep the upper substrate from entering the lower reservoir.

27. Push the burlap divider into the developing bed, so it reaches the mud pellets.

28. Fill the developing bed with extended coco chips. Fill to ¼" from the highest point of the liner.

Planting and Decoration

29. Cut an area of burlap that covers the developing bed.

30. Use a few staples to hold the burlap set up.

31. Cut an opening for the bay channel and remove any abundance burlap covering the frame of the bed.

32. Cut openings for transplants.

33. Transplant and mark seedlings utilizing chalk.

34. Immediately water the garden from above in the wake of transplanting to reach the substrate.

35. For the initial two weeks, water the garden from over each couple of days. Try not to utilize the inlet pipe until the plants get the opportunity to send roots to profound into the substrate to get to water alone. Following half a month, the plants ought to be Topable to get to the reservoir beneath and may not require watering for possibly more than seven days relying upon the clay.

36. This garden doesn't utilize a substrate that has an underlying fertilizer charge, so all Nutrients should be given through water-solvent manures during waterings. Watering with a hydroponic Nutrient solution once seven days is regularly adequate to meet Nutrient requirements of crops right now. When adding water to this system, don't quit watering until the system is obviously draining.

Chapter Three: Nutrient Film Techniques(NFT)

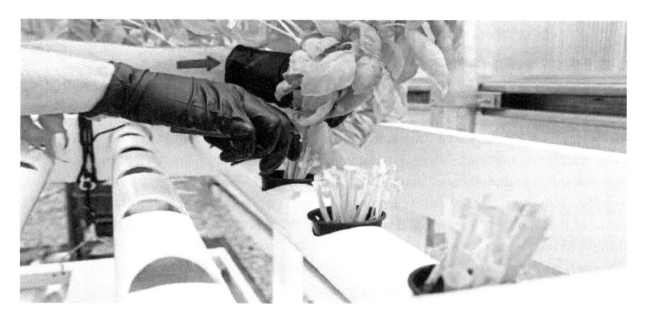

Nutrient Film Techniques (NFT)

Nutrient film method (NFT) is a coursing hydroponic developing style that irrigates plants with a shallow Flow of Nutrient solution in developing channels. NFT is one of the most famous systems for financially developing leafy greens. Perhaps the greatest preferred position is the Capacity to grow a ton of plants on a little Reservoir. NFT is popular with houseTop producers since they can cover the whole roofTop in NFT channels utilizing a small Reservoir that won't surpass the heap conveying limit of the roofTop. A gallon of water weighs 8.34 pounds that implies 240 gallons weighs over a ton! The heaviness of water can rapidly include. Many home garden workers may likewise be stressed over overwhelming reservoirs, particularly inside.

NFT is a famous DIY hydroponic system since it very well may be tweaked from numerous points of view. I've seen NFT directs orchestrated in cascading patterns on walls, in A-frame pyramids, and in spiralling loops. Some DIY NFT systems are more effective than others—it tends to be anything but difficult to let inventive structure dominate and overlook the basics that make an NFT garden fruitful. I urge everybody to explore, yet first, get familiar with the potential constraints and subtleties of NFT plants so you can dodge expensive errors. The achievement of your NFT garden will rely upon crop determination, developing condition, channel length, channel slant, channel shape, and Flow rate.

- **Suitable Locations:** Indoors, exterior, or garden

- **Size:** Medium to enormous

- **Growing Media:** Stone wool

- **Electrical:** Required

- **Crops:** Leafy greens, herbs, and strawberries

Crops

The most popular crops for NFT are leafy greens, herbs, and strawberries. At development, these crops have a respectable root system; however, by and large, insufficient roots to confine Flow in the NFT channel. Roots clogging the channels can be an issue when developing bigger crops like tomatoes, peppers, and cucumbers. Some DIY planters utilize enormous PVC pipes (4 inches or more) or extremely wide drains to oblige the foundations of these bigger crops. Don't hesitate to test; however, when all is said in done, NFT isn't the perfect system for developing enormous crops.

Locations

The Capacity to inundate numerous channels on a little reservoir, without the heaviness of several gallons, makes NFT famous for indoor gardens. NFT is an extraordinary decision for houseTops, study halls, overhangs, and condos. NFT cultivates by, and large have a decent level covering, which is extraordinary for develop lights. It is some of the time precarious to develop plants of different statures under a grow light since some may get a ton of light while hindering the light for different crops, yet this is once in a while an issue with indoor NFT gardens.

NFT Channels

The channels in this build are made from 2-inch PVC pipe with 2-inch net pots. Other well known DIY choices are 3-inch PVC pipe, downpour canals, and vinyl fence posts. In the case of utilizing waterways, it is ideal for making a canal spread to stay away from green growth development in the channel. Flat- bottom channels like drains and fence present now and again direct water on the sides of the channel rather than straightforwardly down the centre. This redirection of the water to the sides makes it hard to get great contact between the seedling and the Irrigation Flow. Drains with grooves on the base some of the time relieve this issue by spreading the Flow equitably along the bottom of the channel.

The length of the channel is a significant thought. Most business NFT channels extend from 4 to 15 feet. Longer channels some of the time have issues with hanging and should be upheld at a few focuses. A listing channel makes territories of dormant water Flow, which can prompt diminished oxygen accessible to the roots, an ascent in water temperature, and an expansion in the possibility of root illnesses.

Long directs are not suggested in warm atmospheres since they regularly have issues with heat development. The water will spend quite a while in a long channel before coming back to the reservoir, and this expanded time in the channel prompts expanded temperatures in the Nutrient solution. Garden workers in warm atmospheres should centre on channels 8 feet and shorter, except if utilizing a water chiller or another technique for cooling the Nutrient solution.

The slant of an NFT channel is additionally significant for constraining warmth development in the Nutrient solution and staying away from the stagnation of the Nutrient solution inside channels. A slant of 1 to 4 per cent is satisfactory; 2 to 3 per cent is commonly the incline utilized in business systems. The system worked right now a 1-inch drop over a 4-foot (48-inch) channel to make a 2-per cent incline.

Flow Rate

Most NFT gardens focus on a Flow pace of ½ to 1 litre for every channel every moment. I've discovered upgrades in plant development with Flow rates up to 2½ litres per channel every moment. To quantify the Flow rate per channel, expel the Irrigation line to that channel and divert it to an estimating cup. Either measure precisely how much water Flows from that line in one moment or discover to what extent it takes to fill 1 litre and utilize that number to compute the Flow rate every moment. The Irrigation area in the Equipment part subtleties the procedure for figuring the least pump crop to meet the Flow rate requirements in a hydroponic garden. But since it is such significant data, I am rehashing it here.

The central point to consider while choosing a water pump are conveyance stature, target Flow rate, and crop tube size. Most systems basically need a pump sufficiently Great to convey water to particular tallness. For instance, a cultivator choosing a pump for a flood and channel system can fundamentally concentrate on whether that pump has most extreme conveyance tallness more prominent than the good ways from the pump outlet to flood plate.

A few systems perform best when water is conveyed at an objective Flow rate. Two or three systems that rely upon target Flow rates are NFT and aeroponics. For these systems, it is critical to consider how conveyance tallness will affect the Flow rate. A pump that conveys 600 gallons for every hour (GPH) at 4 feet high just conveys 200 GPH at 10 feet high. The number of producers will likewise affect the Flow rate. It is commonly better to choose a pump that might be marginally overwhelmed than a pump that could be underelectricityed. It is conceivable to decrease Flow utilizing valves, yet it is preposterous to expect to expand Flow.

Example: A NFT system has an objective Flow pace of 15 GPH per channel. The system has 20 channels. This implies the pump must have the option to convey 15 GPH to 20 channels, so 15 GPH × 20 channels for a sum of 300 GPH. Also, the channels are 2 feet over the pump outlet.

Materials

Frame

2   2 × 6" × 8' amble

2   2 × 4" × 8' amble

1 gal. White water-based latex

preliminary, sealer, and stain-blocker (KILZ 2 LATEX)

1 lb.   #10 × 2½" exterior screws

1 lb.   #8 × 1¼" exterior screws

Channels

3   2" PVC, 10'

22   2" net pots

Irrigation

4   2" PVC tee

6   2" PVC end Top

4   ¾" elbow

11'   ¾" dark vinyl tubing 3'   ¼" dark vinyl tubing

1   Zip tie

9   ¾" EMT ties

1   ¾" gasket

4   ¼" straight twofold spiked connectors

1   Submersible water pump, 550 GPH

Optional Lighting for Lower Level

1   4' six-tube T5 develop light

1   Light holder

Tools

Paint roller and additionally paintbrush

Round observed Deburring instrument Drill

Hacksaw

Step boring apparatus with ⅛" increases from ¼" to 1⅜"

SIZING tape Permanent marker 2¾" opening saw boring apparatus

Rafter square (additionally called a speed square)

Level

Drill bit matching screws

Sawhorses with clamps

2" opening saw boring apparatus

Irrigation line gap punch

Heavy-obligation scissors

Safety equipment

Work gloves

Eye protection

Lumber and PVC Preparation

Most reservoirs that sell lumber offer to slice the Lumber to explicit measurements whenever mentioned. Some home improvement reservoirs will cut PVC as well. Solicitation the measurements recorded in the means beneath to avoid crafted by cutting the Lumber or potentially PVC to decrease the measure of work and apparatuses required.

1. Wearing work gloves and Eye protection, cut the two 2 × 6" × 8' boards into the accompanying lengths:

• One board into two 4' segments

• One board into two 2'6¾" segments

2. Cut the two 2 × 4" × 8' boards into four 4' segments.

Final lengths and amounts of cut Lumber:

2   2 × 6" × 4' boards

2   2 × 6" × 2'6¾" boards

4   2 × 4" × 4' boards

3. Paint the Lumber before assembly.

4. Cut the 2" PVC to make the accompanying lengths. Clean the frames of the cuts with a deburring device.

4   3'7" segments

3   2¼" segments

1   4" fragment

1   3" fragment

¾" grommets

Assemble the Manifold

The complex will Assemble the waste from the NFT channels. Before sticking any of the segments together, watch that the absolute length of the complex is under 27½ inches.

If it is longer, the 3-inch PVC segments can be cut down to 2¼ inches. The focal point of the tees ought to be 5 inches separated. Channels can be separated nearer or opposite the than 5 inches separated, however this dividing works extraordinary for lettuce and basil. The finish of the complex with the 4-inch PVC segments will be utilized for a ¾-inch seepage line. A ¾-inch elbow will be embedded into the PVC, and another ¾-inch elbow will guide the Flow to the Reservoir. Watch that there is sufficient space to fit elbows before sticking.

Some PVC tees and Tops are longer or shorter than others, so there might be a few changes explicit to your Materials. Just continue once the complex Assembled without a stick is under 27½ inches long, the tees have 5-inch separating at their focuses, and there is adequate space on the 4-inch PVC fragment to fit the ¾-inch elbows.

5. The four 2" PVC tees are associated with the 2¼" PVC segments. Paste the tees, so they all lay level on a surface.

6. One end Top interfaces with the tees utilizing the 4" PVC portion and the other Top associates utilizing the 3" PVC segments.

7. The finish of the complex with the 4" PVC segments will be used for the ¾" waste line. A ¾" elbow will be embedded into the PVC, and another ¾" elbow will guide the Flow to the reservoir. Watch that there is sufficient space to fit these before penetrating. Gradually drill the PVC and occasionally check to check whether the gap is sufficiently enormous to hold the grommet. Most ¾" grommets fit in a 15/16" to 1" opening.

8. Fit the grommet cosily into the opening in the PVC complex and addition one of the

¾" elbows.

Assemble the Frame

9. Place the complex on one of the 2 × 6" × 2'6¾" boards. There ought to be at any rate 1½" of space from the end Tops to the 6" frames of the board. The complex ought to be ½" from one of the 2'6¾" frames and 2½" from the other 2'6¾" frame. With a marker, follow the parts of the bargains" tees.

10. Repeat stage 9 on the other 2 × 6" × 2'6¾" board. Make sure to follow the 2" tees close the 2'6¾" frame of the board. It is the situating of these circles that will decide the incline of the NFT channels.

11. Use the 2¾" gap boring apparatus to make openings at the followed Locations in the 2'6¾" boards. Wipe off any sawdust from the boards.

12. Position this 2'6 ¾" boards over the reservoir. Position the 2 × 6" × 4' boards over these, running the length of the reservoir. These will be utilized to manage the situating of the help legs.

13. Use the square and level when securing the help legs to the reservoir. It is significant that these legs are straight upstanding and not inclining. Utilize two 2½" screws to verify the legs into position.

14. Fasten the 2 × 6" × 4' boards to the help legs. The Top frame of the 4' boards ought to be flush with the highest point of the legs.

15. Mark the situation for the 2'6¾" Rafter s. The top finish of the NFT channels will experience a Rafter 5¼" from the finish of the 4' boards, and the low finish of the NFT channels will experience a Rafter 6¼" from the opposite finish of the 4' boards.

16. Arrange the 2'6¾" Rafters, so one side has the penetrated gaps toward the base, and the opposite side has the drill bit holes toward the Top. Secure the Rafter s with just one screw close to the highest point of the frame. It will be essential to be able to change the point of this board while embedding the PVC channels. Later they will be verified into place with a subsequent screw.

17. Insert the 3'7" PVC segments into the Rafter s. These will be developing channels.

18. Attach the complex to the 3'7" PVC channels. The ¾" seepage elbow ought to be on the lower side of the complex. Try not to stick it yet.

19. Mark the situation of the net pots in the channels. The net pots right now 6" separated inside the direction and are orchestrated in a checkerboard example to make extra space between plants from adjacent channels.

20. Takedown the channels from the casing. Utilize a sawhorse with clasps to hold the diverts set up while penetrating gaps for the net pots. Utilize the 2" gap boring tool. Make sure to keep the drill straight and position the bit in the PVC pipe. If the drill is askew or at a frame, it can cut into the side mass of the PVC pipe.

21. Use the deburring apparatus to clean the penetrated gaps.

22. Glue the drill bit d channels to the complex. Keep the openings upstanding!

23. Insert the channels with connected complex go into the Rafter s. 24 Position the end Tops on the channels; however, don't stick them into place.

25 Mark positions for the ¼" water conveyance lines.

26. Drill a little gap in the stamped areas and utilize the deburring instrument to open up the hole until it is wide enough for a ¼" vinyl tube. The ¼" cylinder ought to be held firmly set up

when embedded. It might be simpler to expel the channels and complex from the frame to penetrate the gaps.

Assemble the Irrigation System

27. The fundamental water conveyance line to the channels is a ¾" vinyl tube appended to a submersible pump in the Reservoir. The ¾" conveyance line can be approached the channels along one of the help legs. Utilize an elbow to coordinate the cylinder over the Rafter. End the line going over the Rafter with a ¾" elbow. This elbow connects to a short 4" portion of ¾" tube that is held firmly collapsed into equal parts with a zip tie. This zip bind can be expelled to clear out the Irrigation line during system cleanouts. The elbow toward the end permits the garden worker to coordinate the water away from the system during a cleanout. Attach the ¾" water conveyance line set up with ¾" EMT ties and 1¼" screws.

28. Use the Irrigation line opening puncture the highest point of the flat

¾" tube. Nutrient the ¼" twofold thorned connectors into these openings.

29. With scissors, cut four 8" segments of ¼" dark vinyl tubing. Join one finish of the cylinders to the ¼" twofold thorned connectors and Nutrient the opposite end into the PVC channel. The cylinder ought to be situated in the channel, so the Flow is coordinated down the channel.

30. Place the end Tops on the channels. These end Tops ought not to be stuck into place; it is ideal to be able to expel them, later on, to encourage cleaning and make Troubleshooting potential issues simpler.

31. Create the ¾" waste line by interfacing the elbow in the complex to another ¾" elbow utilizing a little area of ¾" tubing. This will coordinate the seepage descending. It additionally makes it simple to run the ¾" seepage line along one of the help legs. The seepage line should arrive at the base of the reservoir. The submersible pump and waste line are situated at corners inclining to one another so the water will flow over the reservoir when water circles through the channels.

32. Modify the 2" net pots by removing the base. This will guarantee the seedlings have contact with the Nutrient solution and it makes expelling the plants from the pots simpler during harvest.

33. Add the second screw to the Rafter s to safely attach them to the 2 × 6" × 4' boards.

34. If this NFT garden is worked over the Floating Raft garden, including a develop light for the floating raft garden can be a massive assistance. It is conceivable to create plants in the Raft

system without including a grow light; however, development might be moderate and extended. This plan utilizes a 4' six-tube T5 light.

Planting and Cropping

35. Seedlings ought to have roots obviously rising up out of the base of the plug before being transplanted into an NFT channel.

36. Some crops, similar to basil and different herbs, can be Assembled on various occasions. This is incredible and by and large not an issue, however once in a while, the foundations of these plants can develop so gigantic that they will begin to confine the Flow inside the channels.

37. Many NFT plant specialists like to reap living plants. The entire plant with roots connected can be put away inside in some water, and the leaves are pulled off varying. This is an extraordinary method to impart your Assemble to companions while keeping the produce new.

38. Net pots can be reused. Evacuate roots to be treated the soil and spare the pots. The pots can be washed, flushed, and reused.

Troubleshooting

Clogged up channel

• Check to check whether roots are clogging the channel. Assemble crops if necessary, to open up the channel.

• Check to check whether an extended clay pellet or other substrate is obstructing waste line.

Clogged up Irrigation lines

• If utilizing ball valves (shutoff valves), close off Flow to all ¼" Irrigation lines with the exception of the Clogged up line. If the weight doesn't evacuate obstruct, unfurl a paper clasp and push it down Irrigation line to loosen any debris clogging line. If the line is as yet Clogged up, supplant the line with new ¼" tube. If a line is as however Clogged up, supplant the ¼" double barbed connector.

Chapter Four: Top Drip Systems/Aeroponics

Top Drip System

TOP DRIP IS A HYDROPONIC procedure that incorporates a broad scope of garden plans, all with one comparable element: Irrigation lines convey water to the highest point of the substrate. Sometimes the Irrigation lines are joined to Flow rate controllers that make a moderate drip, in this manner Top drip. One of the more popular varieties of Top drip is Dutch basins. Dutch bottles are shut base pots with a solitary waste site. This waste site is marginally raised from the base of the bucket, so it tends to be set up to deplete into a variety pipe that coordinates the pre-owned Nutrient solution back to the reservoir to be recycled.

• **Suitable Locations:** Indoors, exterior, or garden

- **Size:** Medium to huge

- **Growing Media:** Perlite or clay pellets

- **Electrical:** Required

- **Crops:** Leafy greens and huge blooming crops, including tomatoes, cucumbers, and peppers

Crops

Dutch buckets are generally utilized for enormous blossoming crops like bounces, tomatoes, peppers, cucumbers, and eggplant. Huge numbers of these huge crops can be developed for a year or more in a Dutch bucket. Leafy greens and herbs can be developed in Dutch basins, yet most hydroponic garden workers like to exploit their cans by growing huge blooming crops.

Locations

Dutch basin gardens are ordinarily exterior or in gardens in light of the fact that the crops can get immense. Numerous plant specialists utilizing Dutch cans Install a trellis system by the bottles so plant development can be coordinated upward and oversaw in a space-productive way. Utilizing Dutch cans inside is a choice. However, the development needs to be overseen such that utilizes develop lights. Some develop lights can be Installed vertically to light a vertically trellised crop. Most indoor plant specialists set up a flat trellis and weave the plant development on a level plane to make even tallness covering. A pleasant level covering is incredible for developing lights since it makes negligible concealing of different plants and augments the utilization of light.

MATERIALS & TOOLS

Frame

1   2 × 12" × 8' lumber

1 gal. White water-based

latex primer, sealer, and stain blocker (KILZ 2 LATEX)

1 lb.   #10 × 2½"

exterior screws

Buckets

2	Square bucket
1	¾" elbow
1	¾" gasket

Substrate

Extended clay pellets

Irrigation

4'	1½" PVC
1	1½" elastic Top with cinch
1	1½" elastic

elbow with cinches

| 2 | 1½" EMT |

2-gap lash 20 gal. Reservoir

5'	¾" dark vinyl tubing
1	Submersible water pump, 550 GPH
3	¾" EMT 2-gap lash
1	Zip tie
2	¼" twofold pointed connectors
4'	¼" dark vinyl tubing
1	Outlet clock

Tools

Circular saw Hacksaw

Paint roller as well as paintbrush

Level

Beam square Tape measure

Permanent marker Drill

3/16" boring tool

Drill bit matching screws

Step boring tool with ⅛" increases from ¼" to 1⅜"

Deburring instrument 2" gap boring tool

Uncompromising scissors Irrigation line gap

punch

Optional

Trellis netting, 5 × 30',

3½" work

2   Ball valves (stop valves)

2   Irrigation stakes

Safety equipment

Work gloves

Eye protection

Frame Assembly and Bucket Preparation

Bottle choice is significant. The perfect bottle is square and there ought to be in any event a 2-inch hole between the cans when stacked into one another. The buckets right now got for nothing from the pastry kitchen segment of a market. Numerous pastry shops get their crude fixings in large square bottles.

There are numerous approaches to make frame Assembleing simpler. Most reservoirs that sell stumble offer to slice the wood to specific measurements whenever mentioned. Request the dimensions recorded in the means underneath to avoid crafted by slicing the Lumber and decrease the number of Tools required.

The casing should slant toward the reservoir. A few cultivators like to utilize ash obstructs as supports for the bottles, or a blend of soot squares and wood. Top drip basins can get substantial, so ensure the casing is fit for supporting a great deal of weight.

1. Wearing work gloves and eye protection, cut the 2 × 12" × 8' board into the accompanying lengths:

2 × 12" × 16"

2 × 12" × 16¼"

2 × 12" × 2'

2. Remove any names from the cans.

3. Paint the Lumber before assembly. The external basins can be painted as well, whenever wanted. The internal can in the twofold Dutch bucket shouldn't be painted.

4. Measure and mark waste openings in the inward bucket and drill the gaps utilizing the 3/16" boring tool. The Top bottle ought to be quick draining.

5. Build the frame utilizing the 16" and 16¼" boards as legs. The shorter help leg is nearest to the reservoir to make an incline toward the Reservoir and is situated 7½" from the frame of the 2 × 12" × 2' board to make a shade. Utilize the level and square to Assemble the casing with the 2½" screws.

6. Keeping the cover of the Top can is Optional. A cover on the Top basin can help decrease green growth development. Make gaps in the Top bigger than the size of the transplants. Most Dutch buckets are fit for developing in any event two plants.

Assemble the Irrigation System

This Irrigation configuration can be adjusted to add more basins to the garden. To extend this garden, increment the length of the casing, the 1½" PVC line, and the ¾" vinyl tubing, and include extra ¼" lines falling off the ¾" vinyl tubing for the extra buckets.

7. Cut the PVC into a 25" segments and a 10" fragment.

8. Check the situating of the bucket and PVC pipe. There ought to be sufficient space on either side of the PVC funnel to secure an EMT lash.

9. Top the finish of the 25" PVC pipe with the 1½" elastic Top. Fix the cinch on the Top.

10. Attach the 1½" elastic elbow to the opposite finish of the 2'1" PVC pipe.

11. Fasten the 25" PVC channel to the frame with the two 1½" EMT ties.

12. Drill a 1" gap for the ¾" waste elbow from the bottle.

13. Use the deburring instrument to clean the penetrated opening. The deburring device can likewise be utilized to augment the opening.

14. Position the ¾" elbow from the lower basin into the PVC pipe.

15. Drill a 2" opening into the reservoir cover to fit the 1½" PVC waste line. Position the opening in the Reservoir so there will be an insignificant curve in the elastic elbow.

16. Attach the 10" PVC pipe area to the 2'1" PVC pipe segment with the elastic elbow.

17. Drill a 1" opening in the reservoir Top for the ¾" dark vinyl tubing.

18. Connect the ¾" dark vinyl tubing to the submersible pump set inside the reservoir.

19. Position the ¾" dark vinyl tubing along the frame of the 2 × 12" × 2' board.

Affix into position utilizing the ¾" EMT lashes.

20. Leave 6" of vinyl tubing after the last EMT tie. Remove the overabundance.

21. Use a zip bind to crimp the finish of the ¾" tube. This zip bind can be expelled to wash out the Irrigation line or to extend the system.

22. Create a little gap in the ¾" tube for the ¼" twofold pointed connector. The hole can be made with an Irrigation line gap punch or the tip of a screw. Start with an exceptionally little opening to maintain a strategic distance from the chance of making the gap excessively huge. If the opening is too enormous, the ¾" cylinder should be supplanted. Addition the ¼" twofold spiked connector into the little opening, and afterwards repeat to include a second ¼" twofold spiked connector. This is like the NFT Irrigation configuration.

23. Fill the bucket with pre-flushed extended clay pellets.

24. Remove the reservoir and hand-water the bucket to wash out any plastic shavings or remaining clay dust on the pellets.

25. Place the Reservoir back set up and in part-load up with water.

26. Cut two 2' segments of ¼" dark vinyl tubing. Associate these ¼" cylinders to the ¼" twofold pointed connectors in the ¾" dark vinyl tubing.

27. Plugin the pump to test the Irrigation. Check for spills in the ¾" tube. If breaks are distinguished at the ¼" twofold pointed connectors, supplant the ¾" tube.

If breaks are distinguished toward the finish of the ¾" tube, fix as well as supplant the zip tie.

28. In this Top drip plan, I utilized ball valves (shutoff valves) and Irrigation stakes. This isn't required; however, it is useful. Ball valves are extraordinary for controlling Flow while associating numerous basins to one pump. The Flow can be confined at bottles close to the pump to try and out the Flow among all the basins.

29. Fully fill the Reservoir, change with manure, and modify the pH if necessary. Append the pump to a clock. This system has worked incredible with 15 minutes on and afterwards 30 minutes off, cycling 24 hours per day. This Irrigation recurrence works in my particular condition, which is extremely radiant and hot. Inside or in cooler conditions it might be gainful to expand the off-time between Irrigation cycles. This system utilizes clay pellets that channel rapidly, so luckily it is hard to over water plants right now structure.

AEROPONICS

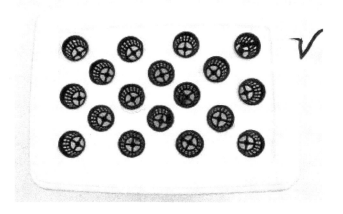

Aeroponics is an exceptionally energizing hydroponic procedure. It offers the potential for rapid development and huge crops while utilizing almost no water. There are two significant classes inside aeroponics: high weight and low weight.

High Pressure: The manufacture direct beneath tells the best way to construct a high-pressure aeroponic garden. Most hydroponic producers consider high-pressure structures when they hear the term aeroponics. A pump is joined to a principle Irrigation line, regularly PVC, and misters are embedded into the PVC line. The pump makes pressure in the PVC pipe, which creates a fine fog. High-pressure aeroponic structures are prevalent for establishing cuttings or "clones." The fine Nutrient solution fog makes an incredible domain for new root development.

Low Pressure: Low-pressure aeroponic gardens don't utilize misters. The aeroponic "fog" is regularly made bypassing the Nutrient solution through punctured plates or potentially making sprinkles close to the plant roots. Low-pressure aeroponic systems by and large have less moving parts and are less inclined to clogging.

Crops

Almost any crop can be developed aeroponically. I've seen papayas grown in aeroponic systems! The most well-known crops for aeroponic systems are leafy greens and herbs, yet don't feel constrained to these alternatives. If developing bigger blooming crops, make sure to consider how the plant will be bolstered. Plants grown in pots can strengthen themselves (to a limited degree) by tying down their underlying foundations to the substrate. Without a substrate, the plant roots don't have a lot of physical help, and a Top-overwhelming plant could lean or fall over if not given support, for example, a vertical or level trellis. Long haul crops likewise have a more noteworthy possibility of confronting a force blackout or a hardware disappointment that could rapidly harm roots or kill plants that may have required numerous long stretches of care.

- **Suitable Locations:** Indoors, exterior, or garden

- **Size:** Small to enormous

- **Growing Media:** Perlite or mud pellets

- **Electrical:** Required

- **Crops:** Leafy greens, herbs, strawberries, and other short crops

Locations

Aeroponics is reasonable for any area. Aeroponic gardens can be little and fit on kitchen counters or be large vertical towers extending more than 15 feet tall. DIY aeroponic gardens can in some cases have issues with breaks and they ought to be tried before being set in a touchy release area.

- **Suitable Locations:** Indoors, exterior, or garden

- **Size:** Small to enormous

- **Growing Media:** Perlite or clay pellets

- Electrical: Required

- Crops: Leafy greens, herbs, strawberries, and other short crops

MATERIALS & TOOLS

Frame

1   23½" L × 16⅞" W × 12¼" H

Capacity tote with Top

18   2" net pot

Irrigation

6'   ¾" PVC pipe

4   ¾" PVC elbow

3   ¾" PVC tee

1   Submersible water pump, 400 GPH PVC stick

10   360° sir, Flow rate 31.4 GPH at 20 PSI

1   Outlet clock

Tools

Permanent marker Drill

2" opening drill bit

Deburring instrument

11/64" brad point boring apparatus

Titanium step boring tool with ⅛" increases from ¼" to 1⅜"

Ratcheting PVC shaper (or hacksaw)

Splash paint (if not utilizing a hazy tote)

Safety Equipment

Work gloves

Eye protection

Set up the Reservoir and Lid

The reservoir determination is significant! It ought to have a tight-fixing Top. When the aeroponic Irrigation turns on, there is a great deal of splashing, so ensure the cover fits firmly to forestall spills. Five-gallon basins additionally work incredible and accompany a tight-plug Top.

1. Spray and paint the reservoir if it isn't dark. Ensure light doesn't arrive at the Nutrient solution since it can support green growth advancement.

2. The cover can be changed to fit a variety of net pot sizes or froth embeds. Froth embeds exceptionally famous for establishing cuttings, and 2" or 3" net pots are extraordinary for developing herbs and leafy greens.

3. Aeroponic systems intended for creating cuttings can fit numerous destinations for froth embeds. These destinations are now and again divided 2½" separated. This aeroponic system will be utilizing net pots divided 3" separated, which is appropriate for a variety of herbs, infant green blends, and some smaller than expected romaine lettuce varieties.

Space the net pots 6" separated to develop full-size lettuce. Imprint the cover with the area of the plant destinations.

4. Wearing work gloves and Eye protection, utilize a 2" gap drill bit to make gaps for the net pots.

5. Clean the frames of the penetrated holes with the deburring instrument.

6. Create an extremely little fold on the cover. This will be utilized for the pump's power cord. Sometimes this flap can be a source of leaks, so another option is drilling a hole in the lid for the cord to pass through and using a foam insert around the cord to cork the drilled hole.

Assemble the Irrigation System

This Irrigation configuration (presented above) can be changed for a variety of Reservoir estimates by modifying the length of the PVC segments and moving the solution of the 360-degree misters.

7. The exact lengths of the PVC segments will rely upon the reservoir and explicit ¾" elbows and tees utilized. Try not to stick any of the segments together until the whole Irrigation system has been test-fitted. Just paste the parts together once they fit well without a stick.

8. Build the middle piece of the Irrigation complex first. It should be sufficiently smaller to fit inside the width of the Reservoir yet there ought to be sufficient space between the tees so an aeroponic mister can be Installed.

9. Cut four PVC segments of equivalent length and connect them to the inside complex. The segments right now 4½" long.

10. Connect the four elbows to the complex.

11. Place a PVC pipe between the elbows and imprint the funnel at the proper length for it to interface the elbows. Cut two segments of this length to interface the two sides.

12. The length of the last PVC segments that will interface the complex to the pump will rely upon the tallness of the Reservoir. It ought to be long enough to put the highest point of the complex inside 5" to 7" of the Top once it is appended to the pump. The PVC complex should fit cosily to the ¾" plug of the pump. If it doesn't fit cosily, attempt another plug that accompanied the pump or use PVC paste to affix PVC channel to the plug.

13. Mark the solution of the 360° misters. This system utilizes a 400 GPH pump. The misters each have a Flow pace of 31.4 GPH. In this way, 400 GPH separated by 31.4 GPH approaches 12.73. For great weight to be guaranteed, ten misters can be used. This pump has a valve to modify Flow rate, so try and include fewer misters than its most extreme to ensure great Flow. The Flow rate can generally be decreased on the pump if there is an excessive amount of weight.

14. Drill openings at the checked spots with the 11/64" drill bit. Curve the 360° misters into the penetrated openings.

15. Place the completely Assembled Irrigation complex and pump in the focal point of the reservoir. Fill the reservoir with water. Try not to fill over the stature of the misters.

16. Place the Top on the reservoir and plug in the pump. Check the conveyance of the misters to ensure all plant locales get water.

17. Plug the pump into a clock. This garden was set to water for 10 seconds each 5 minutes. The Irrigation recurrence will rely upon the age of the crop, nature, the size of the pots, and the clock choice. Numerous aeroponic systems work well when on for 15 minutes and afterwards off for 15 to 45 minutes.

Plant

18. Add the net pots.

19. Amend the reservoir with a hydroponic fertilizer (don't utilize natural hydroponic manure).

Transplant!

Chapter Five: Vertical Gardens

VERTICAL GARDENS COME IN ALL shapes and sizes utilizing both soil and hydroponic developing methods. Vertical gardens are famous for garden workers with restricted space since they can boost the accessible, developing territory in a given impression. Vertical gardens are likewise famous as living art instalments. It is progressively basic to go to a bar, café, office, or school and see a vertical garden utilized as a palatable art instalment.

There are a couple of contemplations to remember while picking a vertical garden. Firstly, not all crops are appropriate for this creation technique. Huge, Top-substantial crops like tomatoes, eggplant, and peppers might not have the help they require whenever developed in a vertical garden. Most vertical hydroponic systems are most appropriate for leafy greens, herbs, and strawberries. The second significant thought is the light necessity of the picked crop. Vertical gardens are famous for having light issues if inadequately structured or situated. Once inA a while vertical systems cast conceal on lower crops. Lacking light for smaller crops may not be an issue during summer when there is a great deal of light; however, in lower light conditions, this can be an issue.

Despite the fact that this book centres around hydroponics, hydroponics isn't the main choice while choosing a vertical garden structure. The garden appeared in the accompanying undertaking could without much of a stretch be altered to utilize a preparing blend and get hand waterings. I for one find that investing the underlying exertion of building a hydroponic system pays off over the long haul since I don't need to make sure to water my plants, however to every howdy or her own—this is DIY! Here is a portion of the basic vertical hydroponic garden solutions.

Aeroponic Towers

Aeroponic systems can be either low or high weight. A high-pressure aeroponic vertical garden will, for the most part, have a principle Irrigation line in an enormous cylinder or square. This primary Irrigation line will have equitably divided foggers or misters that radiate a fine fog for the plant roots situated within the external cylinder or square. These systems require a tolerable measure of weight and can be inclined to clog.

An Irrigation system that utilizes misters or foggers requires the utilization of a Top-notch fertilizer that won't encourage. The producer should likewise be careful of departs and roots falling into the system, in light of the fact that these may separate and obstruct producers.

A low-pressure aeroponic vertical garden will likewise have a fundamental Irrigation in a huge cylinder or square; however, it will just discharge the Nutrient solution at the Top of the garden. The Nutrient solution at that point falls through a progression of plates that scatter the water. Tower Garden is an exceptionally well known low-pressure vertical aeroponic system.

DIY forms of this system are conceivable, yet some of the time is beneficial just to buy a total system.

Drip Towers

Drip towers likewise come in numerous shapes and sizes. They practically all comprise of either a vertical post or pack brimming with an inactive substrate like perlite, coco, or stone wool. The

ZipGrow tower is a vertical drip tower that has increased a great deal of fame in the previous not many years. It utilizes a plastic network and a narrow tangle in a square post.

Flood And Drain Grow Racks

Flood and channel develop racks are a typical vertical system in business ranches. Appeared beneath is a picture of a vertical flood and channel system by Growtainer. Numerous cultivators make their own renditions of these systems. A large portion of these are developed out of metal stockpiling racks, flood tables, and lights. When planning your own flood and channel develop rack, it is essential to incorporate shutoff valves for each level. These valves will assist you with altering the stream to each level so they all fill in generally a similar sum of time. The stature among levels and situation of lights is likewise significant. A large portion of these develop racks have 18 to 24 creeps between levels. I propose utilizing T5 fluorescent or LED bars for lighting. The most well-known issues I see with develop racks are inadequate light and poor wind stream. Probably the best pointer that light levels are low is spindly, stretchy development in seedlings. The seedlings are connecting for all the more light.

Regularly, it is smarter to evacuate spindly seedlings and begin once again. Wind current can likewise help fortify seedlings. A little clasp on fan can tenderly shake the seedlings, urging them to create more grounded stems and better-settled roots. With crops like head lettuce, poor wind current will here and there bring about tip consume.

Rotating/Ferris Wheel

Rotating hydroponic systems are cool looking, yet for the most part not down to earth. Gardens like the Omega Garden are amusing to take a gander at yet the producers utilizing these systems appear to rapidly lose intrigue. Trouble seeing and getting to the yield, issues with wind stream, water trickling onto leaves, significant expense, high upkeep . . . these are only a couple of the reasons producers forsake rotating hydroponic systems. All things considered, I've had a great deal of fun structure Ferris wheel hydroponic systems. These systems are not intended to streamline creation, increment yield, or diminish work; they are intended to just be tastefully satisfying. Ferris wheel grower can be found at some garden shops and a hunt through online merchants will for the most part bring about a few choices. I've had a go at building two or three Ferris wheel systems and have taken in a couple of exercises in the process. To begin with, moving the Ferris wheel with an engine so the plants can be plunged into a supplement solution can be a migraine. Second, gravity and the heaviness of water are extraordinary for moving plants in a Ferris wheel. Third, use pots that channel rapidly. By and large, stone fleece and additionally perlite are acceptable choices for these systems.

NFT A-FRAME

An NFT A- frame system comprises of NFT diverts orchestrated in an A shape. These systems have advantages and disadvantages. The expert is the capacity to build the quantity of plant destinations in a given impression. The cons are a lopsided conveyance of light and conceivable stream rate issues. On the off chance that you plan on building An outline NFT system, follow similar rules for incline and stream rate as referenced in the NFT venture. Furthermore, use ¼-inch shutoff valves for each channel to adjust stream among all levels. The utilization of ¼-inch shutoff valves is additionally portrayed in the task for the downpour canal garden.

Rain Gutter System

This system is one of the more confounded systems right now.

On the other hand, this system can be thought of as a model for an a lot bigger system.

This system could without much of a stretch be adjusted to have 10-inch-wide channels. It could be numerous levels taller as well. While including increasingly vertical levels, it is imperative to consider pump size.

Larger than usual pumps likewise help decrease the capability of garbage clogging up the irrigation lines.

Chapter Six: Flood And Drain

FLOOD AND DRAIN

THE FLOOD AND DRAIN TECHNIQUE passes by numerous names, including "back and forth movement" and "ebb and flood." These names all depict the Irrigation strategy utilized right now. A Nutrient solution is pumped to flood a develop plate and afterwards its channels.

This is like the media bed configuration shrouded in the past segment. However, flood and channel gardens don't fill the develop bed with a substrate. Flood and channel plants by and large use pots loaded up with a hydroponic substrate or stone wool squares.

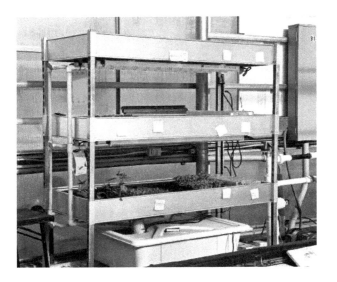 

Crops

The flood and channel garden appeared in the guide underneath can without much of a stretch be changed for anything from microgreens to huge blossoming crops. A flood and channel garden can develop almost any crop with a couple of changes in accordance with Irrigation recurrence, pot size, substrate determination, and flood tallness (channel stature).

Locations

Appropriate for any area. This garden will have comparable issues as other garden structures whenever put exterior and presented to overwhelming precipitation, the essential issue being the washing endlessly and weakening of the Nutrient solution.

• **Suitable Locations:** Indoors, exterior, or garden

• **Size:** Small to huge

- **Growing media:** Perlite, extended clay pellets, stone wool, or coco coir

- **Electrical:** Required

- **Crops:** Any crop contingent upon pot size

VARIATIONS

The assemble control shows a few flood and channel varieties. Here are only a couple of approaches to adjust this garden structure:

• Change pot size. Bigger pots are extraordinary for huge blooming crops. Numerous little pots may be progressively sensible for leafy greens and herbs.

• Change pot cloth. Plastic pots are incredible; however, they can Sometimes lose substrate through waste gaps. This free substrate would then be able to stop up Irrigation lines.

Texture pots are ideal for flood and channel gardens since they make it about difficult to lose substrate. The texture permits the Nutrient answer for rapidly arrive at the plant, and afterwards, it depletes quickly, giving the roots access to air and forestalling overwatering.

• Change the substrate. Extended mud pellets are incredible on the grounds that they are hard to overwater and are reusable. Coco is another extraordinary alternative; it holds more water,

Flood and channel is a famous structure for vertical gardens on the grounds that the develop beds can be stacked on a rack with one reservoir at the base for all the levels.

So Irrigation recurrence ought to be balanced appropriately. Other famous alternatives incorporate perlite, peat, and stone wool. Fine-finished substrates like coco, peat, and little perlite are regularly best in texture pots to abstain from losing substrate from the pots' seepage gaps.

• Change develop bed size. Pre-assembled flood and channel plate come in numerous sizes, by and large running from 1 to 4 feet wide and 2 to 12 feet in length. DIY develop beds can be as large or as little as you need. A develop bed can be built from solid blending plate, middle mass compartments (IBC totes), plastic stockpiling totes, dish tubs, or even wood with a plastic liner (like the wicking bed structure). Whatever is picked, ensure the plate can be adjusted to incorporate a fill plug that is flush, or almost flush, with the base of the plate and a waste plug that is raised over the surface. Most flood and channel plans place the seepage plug around 33% the tallness of the chose pots.

MATERIALS & TOOLS

Reservoir and Grow Bed

1   14" L × 11" W × 3¼" H

plastic tote

1   14.7" L × 10.6" W × 9.1" H

plastic tote (4 gal.) Scotch tape

Shower paint

Irrigation

11"   5/16" dark vinyl tubing 4"   ½" dark vinyl tubing

1   Submersible water pump,

40 GPH

1   Outlet clock

Substrate and Pots*

2   6" square pot

or on the other hand

4   5" square pot

or on the other hand

1   2-gal. texture pot

or on the other hand

5   3" net pot

or on the other hand

Grodan An OK 36/40 3D squares (for microgreens)

Tools

Drill

Step boring tool with ⅛" increases from ¼" to 1⅜"

Hot glue gun

Rock-solid scissors 2¾" gap saw drill bit

Safety Equipment

Work gloves

Eye protection

Set up the Reservoir and Grow Bed

Picking a develop bed and reservoir that fit well together is basic. The base of the develop bed should fit inside the Reservoir, and the lip of the develop bed should hang over the frame of the reservoir.

1. Add a segment of tape on the reservoir. Overlay the finish of the tape under the base. This tape will be evacuated subsequent to painting to make a survey window into the Reservoir to check water tallness.

2. Spray and paint the develop bed, develop bed Top, and Reservoir. Ensure they are completely dark, so light doesn't enter the reservoir. If light enters the Reservoir, it can prompt green growth development. I utilized two layers of writing slate splash paint on this garden.

3. Remove the tape once the splash paint dries to make a survey window.

4. Wearing work gloves and eye insurance, drill a 5/8" and a ⅜" opening in the develop bed.

Assemble the Irrigation System

5. Insert the 11" portion of the 5/16" dark vinyl tubing into the ⅜" opening in the develop bed. Utilize the Hot glue gun to affix the 5/16" tube set up. The 5/16" cylinder ought to be flush with the exterior of the develop bed.

6. Insert the 4" portion of ½" dark vinyl tubing into the ⅝" gap in the build bed. It shouldn't be stuck into position. The tallness of the ½" cylinder will be balanced dependent on substrate and pot determination.

7. Connect the 5/16" cylinder to the submersible pump.

8. Fill the reservoir with water.

9. Position the pump on the base of the reservoir and spot the develop bed over the reservoir.

10. Turn on the pump. Water should fill the develop bed and channel from the ½" tube.

11. Turn the pump off, and water should deplete once more into the reservoir through the pump.

Planting and Harvesting Microgreens

12. Prepare the stone wool by washing it in Nutrient solution.

13. Remove plugs varying for the stone wool sheet to fit the develop bed.

14. Some microgreen seed bundles will give a suggested seeding thickness.

15. Gently fog the microgreen seeds. Clouding the seeds twice every day for the initial 3 to 5 days will support germination.

16. Most microgreens are prepared to Assemble the following 10 to 15 days. A few varieties are slower developing and expect 3 to about a month prior to they are ready to reap.

17. Many microgreen varieties can be reaped on numerous occasions. Cut the young plants over their lowermost leaves to offer them a chance to regrow.

Chapter Seven: Equipment/Irrigation

Equipment

THE EQUIPMENT YOU'LL NEED FOR a developing hydroponic system depends, obviously, on what sort of system you need to make. Aside from the essential systems, hydroponics, for the most part, incorporates a pump to recycle the blend of water and fertilizer. The recycling water is significant on the grounds that it is through the development and at times an airstone with tubing, that oxygen from the surrounding air is provided to the fluid and afterwards to the plants. These pumps, alongside the tubing and joining connectors, are the core of the system and likely the most significant gear you will purchase.

Irrigation

Irrigation is only an extravagant word for watering, yet when you are discussing a developing hydroponic system, characterizing it can get dubious. Regardless of whether you consider Irrigation giving sustenance or giving a system, the gear you have to make the Irrigation work truly comes down to a couple fundamental things: a pump (with or without a channel) to move and circle the water through the system, and a progression of cylinders to pass on the fluid.

Water Pumps

The central point to consider while choosing a water pump are conveyance stature, target Flow rate, and crop tube size. Most systems essentially need a pump incredible enough to convey water to a particular stature. For instance, a cultivator choosing a pump for a flood and channel system can basically concentrate on whether that pump has a most extreme conveyance stature more noteworthy than the good ways from the pump outlet to flood plate. A few systems perform best when water is conveyed at an objective Flow rate.

Two or three systems that rely upon target Flow rates are NFT and aeroponics. For these systems, it is imperative to consider how conveyance tallness will affect the Flow rate. A pump that conveys 600 gallons for every hour (GPH) at 4 feet high just conveys 200 GPH at 10 feet high. The number of producers will likewise affect the Flow rate. It is commonly better to choose a pump that might be somewhat overwhelmed than a pump that could be under electrified. It is conceivable to decrease Flow utilizing valves, yet it is beyond the realm of imagination to expect to expand Flow.

Air Pumps

Air Pumps are basically used to circulate air through however they can likewise be successful for keeping Nutrients w blended in a reservoir. Circulating air through the Nutrient solution can build the disintegrated oxygen. In spite of the fact that plants produce oxygen, they likewise use oxygen to play out dean variety of errands. One of these assignments is moving water through a filtration procedure in the roots. If a plant doesn't have sufficient oxygen around its underlying foundations, at that point the plant will start to wither in the light of the fact that it can't play out the errand of moving water through the filtration procedure and up to the leaves. Expanding oxygen in the root zone frequently builds crop and improves plant wellbeing.

Air Pumps are appraised via wind Flow estimated in litres every moment (L/min). The objective litres every moment for each hydroponic system relies upon numerous variables, including reservoir size, water temperature, crop, and crop age. As opposite as I can tell, 1 L/min per 5 gallons is commonly adequate for most applications.

Air Stones

Air Pumps convey air through air stones, which arrive in a variety of shapes and sizes.

Airstone inclinations change significantly by the producer. I, for one, lean toward adaptable air stones and round air stones with base suction. There are different approaches to circulate air through a Nutrient solution other than vacuum apparatus with air stones or water pumps with venturi connections. Falls or cascades are regularly the sole strategies for circulating air through Nutrient solutions in NFT systems.

Other further developed strategies incorporate ozone age and fluid oxygen infusions.

Tubing

Not all Irrigation tubing is the equivalent. Customary Irrigation tubing utilized in finishing is frequently solid and hard to use in most hydroponic applications. Dark vinyl tubing is commonly the standard decision for hydroponic Irrigation since it is adaptable, is solid, and effectively associates with the standard plugs utilized in hydroponic gardens. The most widely recognized sizes for dark vinyl tubing are ¼, 5/16, ½, ¾, and 1 inch.

Clear tubing isn't suggested for Irrigation lines. There is consistently the potential for green growth development when the Nutrient solution is presented to light. Clear tubing can be a problem area for green growth and is hard to clean once green growth creates. Clear tubing is well known in aquariums in light of the fact that it is almost imperceptible and is all the more tastefully satisfying. If a style is not a significant concern, ¼-inch dark tubing will work similarly just as ¼-inch clear tubing.

Plugs

Flood and channel plugs permit DIY cultivators to make their own flood plate from family unit Materials like plastic stockpiling totes. For the most part, these plugs arrive in a set that incorporates a ½-inch fill plug, a ¾-inch channel plug, expansions, and two screen plugs.

One of the most helpful Irrigation plugs in DIY hydroponics is grommets. They can change PVC pipes, plastic totes, buckets, and more into hydroponic developing regions or reservoirs. Grommets make a watertight seal around Irrigation plugs. Normally accessible in ½ or ¾ inch.

Tubing connectors Topacity and look particularly like the pipes connectors that anybody with experience doing home pipes is acquainted with utilizing (aside from, obviously, that they are a lot littler).

A 2' flexible air stone

Two-outlet air pump

This exploded view of a 400 GPH pump shows the mesh filter, adjustable intake, impeller, suction cups, and two outlet attachments.

Chapter Eight: Pots And Tray

Net pots can be square or roundabout and by and broad range from 2 to 10 inches wide. This book centers around utilize for 2-and 3-inch net pots, the most usually used net pot measures in DIY hydroponic systems.

Circular plastic pots are commonly the most straightforward to discover.

Square plastic pots can help expand the space in a hydroponic garden by evacuating all holes between pots. Square pots are a famous alternative in develop plate since they can be stuffed in firmly.

Grow bags have been utilized in business ranches for quite a while and are beginning to advance into home gardens. They can be hard to reuse; however, they are unquestionably perhaps the least expensive choice for a pot. The side dividers of developing sacks can be moved down to alter the volume of the pot. Despite the fact that the pack may look square when unfilled, it rounds out to be a chamber.

Square pots are great for using space efficiently.

Low-cost grow bag

Fabric pots are incredible for hydroponics since they are fast draining; however, don't have enormous gaps that can let out the substrate. They are ideal for flood and channel systems since it is simple for the water to drench into the substrate and afterwards channel rapidly. Texture pots are anything but difficult to reuse as well! Just vacant out the substrate, turn the pack back to front, let it dry, and get over any residual flotsam and jetsam. They can even be placed in a clothes washer for a profound clean.

Terracotta pots are not usually found in hydroponics, yet that doesn't mean they can't be utilized. Terracotta pots used in gardens are permeable, permitting air and water to go through the dividers, qualities like a textured pot. Unlike a fabric pot, terracotta is overwhelming and delicate.

Classic terracotta pots

Chapter Nine: Substrates And Growing Media

Hydroponic garden workers have a decision between high hazard with quick development and generally safe with more slow growth. The choice is principally founded on the porosity of the substrate and the Capacity of the roots to relax. One of the most widely recognized slip-ups made by new garden workers is overwatering. In an overwhelming soil or a poor-draining pot, an overabundance of water can suffocate the plant. Despite the fact that plants make oxygen, they likewise require oxygen.

The roots particularly need oxygen to play out a basic advance in the take-up of water and Nutrients. Without oxygen in the root zone, the plant can't take-up water, and the highest point of the plant begins to shrivel. It is irrational to see a plant shrivelling when sitting in water. Overabundance water can likewise expand the opportunity of root illness.

Hydroponic planters can choose substrates that hold next to no water to build the oxygen accessible to the roots; however, this requires a visit or persistent Irrigation. A few garden workers want to diminish the number of Irrigation cycles required by utilizing a substrate that holds more water. A substrate that contains more water includes some protection from electricity blackouts, pump disappointments, and other potential wellsprings of deferrals in Irrigation. A plant developed in an exceptionally permeable substrate like mud pellets might be harmed or pass on following several hours of no Irrigation when grown in a warm, bright condition. That equivalent plant developed in coco coir, a substrate that holds significantly more water, might have the option to go several days without Irrigation. Usually the exchange off for this expansion in protection is somewhat more slow development.

Substrates for Starting Seed

This book centres around stone wool and polymer-bound plugs produced using peat greenery and coco coir. There are numerous different alternatives for start substrates, yet these are two of the most learner neighbourly choices since they have a decent water-holding limit yet are hard to overwater.

Stone Wool Commonly called rock wool in the United States, stone wool is made by dissolving basaltic shakes and Rotating the "rock magma" into strands . . . like cotton candy, however opposite less delectable. Disclaimer: Do not eat stone wool! Stone wool is one of the most popular hydroponic substrates in both business and side interest hydroponics.

It has a decent equalization of water maintenance and porosity, which makes it extraordinary for new hydroponic cultivators, who regularly tend to overwater plants. A few substrates are not extremely sympathetic to overwatering. However stone wool, as a rule, will at present Topacity when overwatered—it probably won't have the best development, yet it, as a rule, won't execute the crop. Stone wool is accessible in squares, chunks, and free.

Coconut Coir Also called "coco" coir; coconut coir is a developing substrate produced using the husks of coconuts. It is a well-known substrate for both ordinary and natural hydroponic producers. If coco isn't appropriately washed during handling, it can have elevated levels of salt, which may harm salt-delicate crops. It is a decent practice to wash any coco before utilizing in a hydroponic garden to expel any remaining salts and wash out any tannins that may recolour the Reservoir or developing zone.

Coco Peat A fine coco, in some cases called coco substance or coco dust, coco peat can hold a ton of water. It is regularly utilized as a substitute for or blended in with peat greenery. Coco peat, in contrast to peat greenery, has a beginning pH that is adequate to most vegetables without expecting to include lime. Coco peat, similar to peat greenery, is frequently blended in with perlite or another permeable substrate to help the blend and improve waste.

Coco Chips A thick coco, once in a while called coco bread garnishes, coco chips have a decent equalization of water maintenance and waste. They can be utilized as an independent substrate or fused into a blend. At the point when used as an independent substrate, coco chips may be watered much of the time, like developing in extended mud pellets.

Perlite is made by warming volcanic stone until it pops like popcorn. This extended stone is exceptionally lightweight and has numerous business applications, fundamentally in development. Perlite is utilized in cultivation since it is modest, natural, lightweight, and incredible for circulating air through overwhelming substrates like coco and peat. It comes in numerous sizes, from fine to stout, and can be utilized as an independent hydroponic substrate.

Peat Often called sphagnum peat or sphagnum peat greenery; peat is in part rotted plant matter Assembled from lowlands. It can hold a great deal of water yet is lightweight when dry, ideal for transportation. Peat, for the most part, has an exceptionally low pH around 4. It is regularly blended in with lime to raise the pH to an increasingly satisfactory range for vegetables. Peat can be utilized as an independent substrate; however, it is all the more normally used in a blend in with perlite. Its accessibility is generally constrained to North America, as the Assembling of this nonrenewable asset is seriously limited in the more significant part of the world.

Extended Clay Pellets Sometimes called Hydroton after one of the first producers, and furthermore called LECA (which represents light extended clay total), extended mud pellets are pH nonpartisan, latent, and one of the most popular substrates for both hydroponic and aquaponic media beds. The pores in the pellets can hold some water, yet it is hard to overwater mud pellets since they rush to deplete.

Continuously wash mud pellets before utilizing them in a hydroponic garden.

Reusing Substrates

Waterway rocks and clay pellets can be washed and reused, however different substrates are typically hard to reuse in a hydroponic garden. Most hydroponic plant specialists will blend utilized coco, peat, and perlite into their fertilizer or legitimately into a customary soil garden to improve water maintenance and waste. Some hydroponic plant specialists will likewise separate their pre-owned stone wool 3D squares and segments into little pieces to blend into their conventional soil garden.

Stone wool seedling sheets

Polymer bound plug made of

peat moss and coco coir fiber

Fine coco peat

Coco chips

Chapter Ten: Indoors Equipment

Equipment For Developing Indoors

Although hydroponic gardens don't should be inside, they are by and large connected with indoor developing. Indoor developing may sound simpler on the grounds that there are less erratic occasions like terrible climate and bugs, however indoor garden workers discover there is an entirely different rundown of difficulties. The absolute most normal slip-ups for novice indoor producers are the absence of sufficient wind current, poor temperature control, poor mugginess control, and deficient light. The best possible gear is fundamental to have an effective indoor garden.

Develop Tents

Develop tents give an encased space to ecological controls, lights, and developing systems. Some of the time it very well may be hard to make the best possible developing atmosphere inside, or the perfect developing atmosphere may not be a similar atmosphere you wish to have in the remainder of your indoor space. Plants may like moistness pro segments around 50 to 80 per cent; however, individuals regularly like to be in a stickiness exterior of that extend.

.

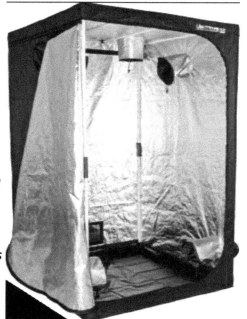

Develop tents arrive in a scope of sizes, from 2' × 2' up to 10' × 20' (and greater!). Ducting ports on develop tents make it simple to set up atmosphere control and to hang lights.

The tents' strong bottoms contain any potential breaks

Develop tents are an extraordinary method to separate the plants in an indoor situation. Other than keeping a different atmosphere from the remainder of the indoor space, a develop tent can keep in the brilliant light required for plant development. It is in some cases profitable to develop lights for 20 hours or more for each day, however, envision individuals living in a little studio condo probably won't be too cheerful having a brilliant light on for 20 hours per day when they're attempting to rest. Develop tents can likewise permit garden workers to contain their irritation the executives' procedures, regardless of whether that is showering or discharging helpful predator bugs to ensure the crop. Develop tents are ideal for leaseholders who don't be able to adjust space for developing. A develop tent can pay for itself when you consider the likely loss of a protection reservoir.

Climate Control

Contingent upon the atmosphere exterior of a develop tent; a plant specialist might have the option to control within an atmosphere with inline fans. Inline fans can be set within, or exterior of the develop tent. There are focal points to both of these solutions. A fumes fan set inside a develop tent is extraordinary for containing crop scents since it ensures any air leaving the develop tent goes through a carbon channel, which traps all smells. This solution is here and there called a negative weight develop room. Air inactively Flows into the develop room from ducting ports as the fumes fan pushes allowing some circulation.

Intake Fans: An admission fan set outwardly can spare significant develop space in the develop tent. Right now, is driven into the develop tent and the fumes latently escape from ducting ports. This positive weight develop room is extraordinary for a bug the executives in light of the fact that the debilitating air makes it hard for nuisances to get into the develop tent. A negative weight develop tent can here and there suck in bugs close to any potential openings, yet a positive weight develops tent will make an outward wind Flow that makes it hard for bugs to enter the develop tent from anyplace however the admission of a fan.

There are some rock-solid air consumption channels, similar to the HEPA channel appeared at left, that can forestall creepy crawlies, microscopic organisms, growths, and dust from going into a develop room.

Note: Grow lights can produce a ton of warmth, and it might be hard to deal with that heat with just ventilation fans. Cooling units committed exclusively to the develop room are once in a while vital for indoor garden workers utilizing exceptionally ground-breaking lights, utilizing different lights, developing in warm atmospheres, or developing temperature-delicate crops.

Airflow

Deficient wind Flow is one of the most widely recognized mix-ups made by novice indoor planters. Fortunately, it is one of the least demanding to cure. Insufficient wind current may bring about spindly, slender plants, frail stems, tip consume, and an improved probability of contagious issues in the crop (i.e., fine buildup). A simple stunt to check whether a develop room has adequate wind current is to take a gander at the leaves to check whether they are unmistakably moving. Unmistakably moving leaves is an indication that there ought to be adequate wind Flow in that area, yet there is consistently the potential for "dead air" spots in a develop room. Oscillating fans can help lessen the potential of these dead air spots.

Inline fans can be placed inside or outside a grow room.

A HEPA filter is capable of preventing insects, bacteria,

fungi, and pollen from entering a grow tent.

Chapter Eleven: Grow Lights

Utilization of fake light to develop plants can be followed back to the 1800s. Develop lights were not constantly a viable alternative, yet in the previous, not many decades, there have been propels in lighting innovation that has utilized develop lights available to interest cultivators with gardens of any size. There are many lighting choices, yet not all are appropriate for your particular developing zone; if you don't mind survey the numerous choices before buying a develop light to evade a conceivably expensive misstep.

Fluorescent: These are likely the most learner well disposed of develop lights.

They are additionally broadly accessible and moderately modest contrasted with other develop lights.

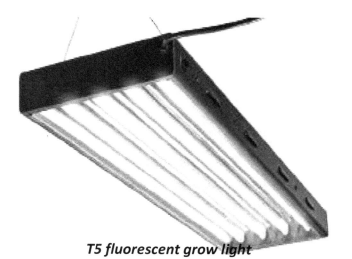

T5 fluorescent grow light

A powerful 1000-watt double-ended(DE)

HPS light is great for greenhouses

and grow rooms with high ceilings.

They devour insignificant electricity and are accessible in a few ranges so that you can grow a wide scope of crops. They may not be perfect for crops that require serious light, for example, peppers. Since they radiate just modest quantities of warmth, they can be set exceptionally near the crop—inside a few inches—which makes them extraordinary for seedlings and young plants.

High-Pressure Sodium (HPS): These are perhaps the least expensive choice for high-force lighting. HPS lights can create a great deal of warmth, which is acceptable in cool situations; however hard to oversee inside without appropriate ventilation or potentially to cool. They frequently are utilized for blossoming crops inside and are extraordinary for giving Nutriental light in gardens. They usually are situated a couple of feet over a crop.

Metal Halide (MH) and Ceramic Metal Halide (CMH): MH and CMH are high-electricity lighting alternatives frequently utilized for vegetative stages but at the same time are equipped for developing blooming crops. Light from MH bulbs seems blue, and numerous plant specialists think that it's lovely to work. The prevailing blue light is additionally useful for electricity smaller development. Most develop light makers are concentrating creation on the fresher, increasingly efficient CMH bulbs rather than the customary MH bulbs.

Light Emitting Diodes (LEDs): LEDs are extremely productive, utilizing negligible electricity to create a great deal of light. They produce next to no warmth comparative with their light crop and are accessible in a wide range of designs, some appropriate for mounting high over the crop and some reasons for setting extremely near the crop. LEDs come in various hues, which can significantly influence plant development. The white LEDs are less productive yet more enjoyable to work under than red and blue LEDs, which cast a purple light that is extraordinary for developing plants, yet a few cultivators find stylishly disappointing.

Extra Light Options: Other alternatives incorporate enlistment lights, plasma lights, and lasers, just as numerous other lighting advances other than the ones recorded previously. A portion of these more current lighting choices can be pricey and may not be appropriate for the starting hydroponic plant specialist. Lighting innovation progresses rapidly, however, and a considerable lot of these alternatives may before long be the standard, similarly as LED lighting is rapidly moving to the bleeding frame among the customary HPS, MH, and fluorescent lighting choices.

Lighting Accessories

Holders Lights can be hung with rope, link, or tie or mounted straightforwardly to a Rafter or the roof. Rope ratchets are exceptionally well known with indoor garden workers since they make moving lights here and there simple.

Develop Room Glasses: Some plant specialists think that its disagreeable to work under the orange light of HPS or the purple light of LED develop lights. Glasses with tinted focal points planned explicitly for these light sources are an incredible method to make it progressively wonderful to work with these develop lights.

Chapter Twelve: Meters

A variety of meters are utilized in most hydroponic systems to screen and help direct the developing condition. The meters measure levels, for example, Nutrient focus and equalization, pH parity, temperature, and light electricity. Some work naturally, and others require the hydroponic garden worker to make and maintain a customary observing project.

Electrical Conductivity (EC)

EC meters are utilized to appraise the manure focus in a Nutrient solution. EC meters are not basic for developing hydroponically, but rather they are certainly one of the most supportive apparatuses. They are accessible in numerous shapes from numerous organizations and in many value ranges. There are some exceptionally ease alternatives accessible that I've seen work for cultivators and hold up for a considerable length of time. A truncheon EC meter is presently a go-to decision for some since it doesn't require adjustment is waterproof and can deal with misuse.

Bluelab truncheon meter (left

and Bluelab pH Pen (right)

A pH control kit with pH indicator

solution, pH up and pH down

pH

In spite of the fact that pH meters are not basic for developing hydroponically, they are incredible for helping hydroponic planters comprehend the condition of their Nutrient solution.

Understanding the pH of the Nutrient solution is additionally helpful when attempting to analyze potential Nutrient inadequacies. However, pH meters are more volatile than EC meters and ought to be manoeuvred carefully and all around kept up, or they can immediately get wrong or just break. Continuously read the guidelines on a pH test to guarantee you effectively adjust it and play out the customary support required to keep the test exact. There is a great deal of variety between pH tests available, and they are not all rise. I've tried numerous pH meters and right now my most loved is the Bluelab pH Pen.

The pH can likewise be tried with a marker solution. These pointer solutions regularly come as a component of a pH control unit that incorporates pH up and pH down solutions. A pH marker solution can give a rough pH, yet it will never be as exact as a pH meter. Numerous new hydroponic producers start with a pH control unit with a pH marker solution since it is a reasonable choice that can take care of business.

Light Intensity

A speculating light force is unbelievably troublesome, if certainly feasible. There are numerous meters accessible to assist plant specialists with checking their light levels to decide if they are adequate, sufficient, or unreasonably extreme for their particular crop.

Lux Meter: Lux meters are commonly the most reasonable meter for estimating light electricity; however, not the best. Lux meters measure light on a scale explicit to how light is seen by the human eye. The human eye is generally touchy to green and yellow, while plants are generally delicate to blue and red. The greater part of the light level suggestions for crops are not founded on lux; they rather utilize photosynthetic photon motion thickness (PPFD), which is estimated by photosynthetically dynamic radiation (PAR) meters.

Standard Meter PAR is an abbreviation for photosynthetically dynamic radiation. Standard light falls inside a wavelength extend that is unmistakable to plants and that plants can use to control photosynthesis. PPFD is an abbreviation for photosynthetic photon transition thickness. PPFD quantifies what number of photosynthetically dynamic photons, estimated in μmol, are arriving in a square meter (m2) each second (s); the unit utilized is μmol/m2/s.

Standard meters are the favoured meter for estimating light electricity in a green situation; however, they will, in general, be more costly than lux meters.

Daily Light Integral (DLI) Meter: A PPFD estimation shows light force per square meter every second. A DLI estimation shows the light electricity conveyed per square meter every day. DLI is an aggregate of all the PPFD readings for each second for the duration of the day. The unit utilized is mol/m2/d. DLI doesn't utilize μmol on the grounds that the number would be enormous: 1 mol is 1,000,000 μmol. DLI is valuable since it measures the light a plant approaches for the duration of the day, not exactly at a solitary minute. Inside it is genuinely simple to figure the DLI with a solitary PPFD estimation on the grounds that the light levels don't vacillate for the duration of the day as they do exterior. For instance, a PPFD perusing inside of 100 μmol/m2/s is changed over to DLI with the accompanying advances:

1. Multiply PPFD by 60 seconds to get absolute μmol per m2 every moment.

Example: 100 μmol/m2/s × 60 seconds = 6000 μmol/m2/minute

2. Multiply this number by an hour to get μmol per m2 every hour.

Example: 6000 μmol/m2/minute × an hour = 360,000 μmol/m2/hour

3. Multiply this number by the number of hours the lights are on; right now, lights are on for 20 hours every day.

Example: 360,000 μmol/m2/hour × 20 hours = 7,200,000 μmol/m2/day

4. Lastly, isolate by 1,000,000 to change over μmol to mol.

Example: 7,200,000/1,000,000 = 7.2 mol/m2/day

Exterior a DLI can be estimated utilizing a DLI meter. A DLI meter is intended to add up to the PPFD estimations for the duration of the day to produce a DLI perusing in mol/m2/day.

The reference diagram beneath depends on personal observations and should just be viewed as a general suggestion.

Crop	Target DLI Range
Microgreens	6–12 mol/m2/day
Leafy Greens	12–30 (by and large 17–25) mol/m2/day

Blooming Crops   17–45 (for the most part 25–35) mol/m2/day

DLI meter that measures total light

delivered in 24 hours using mol/m2/day

Temperature and Humidity Monitoring Equipment

A basic aquarium thermometer is frequently adequate for checking the temperature in a hydroponic reservoir. The objective water temperature for most hydroponic crops is 65° to 70°F; however, it is certainly conceivable to develop solid crops exterior of this range. Most pH and EC meters additionally measure water temperature. Water temperature influences the EC and pH readings, so these meters must factor in the water temperature before giving an exact perusing.

A thermometer with a hygrometer that records day by day high and depressed spots is incredible for observing conditions in a garden or develop room. Garden workers may invest a great deal of energy with their plants; however, they can't be there constantly; a thermometer/hygrometer that screens the high and depressed spots electricity plant specialists to make changes in accordance with a day or night temperatures that they probably won't see when they're in the garden.

Floating thermometer for

monitoring water temperature

CPSIA information can be obtained
at www.ICGtesting.com
Printed in the USA
BVHW011721150421
605033BV00014B/1309